Athletes Who Made a Difference

LEBRON JAMES

Josh Anderson
illustrated by Kristel Becares

Graphic Universe™ • Minneapolis

Graphic Universe™
An imprint of Lerner Publishing Group, Inc.
241 First Avenue North
Minneapolis, MN 55401 USA

For reading levels and more information, look up this title at www.lernerbooks.com.

Main body text set in CCDaveGibbonsLower
Typeface provided by Comicraft

Photo Acknowledgments
The images in this book are used with the permission of: © Michael Zagaris/Getty Images, p. 28 (left); © ANGELA WEISS/Getty Images, p. 28 (right).

Library of Congress Cataloging-in-Publication Data

Names: Anderson, Josh, author. I Becares, Kristel, illustrator.
Title: Lebron James : athletes who made a difference / by Josh Anderson ; illustrated by Kristel Becares.
Description: Minneapolis : Graphic Universe, [2024] I Series: Athletes who made a difference I Includes bibliographical references and index. I Audience: Ages 8–12 years I Audience: Grades 4–6 I Summary: "This graphic biography follows "a kid from Akron, Ohio" as he grows up to become an NBA superstar and an important voice in the fight for racial equality. This is the story of LeBron James"—Provided by publisher.
Identifiers: LCCN 2023051308 (print) I LCCN 2023051309 (ebook) I ISBN 9781728492957 (library binding) I ISBN 9798765627990 (paperback) I ISBN 9798765631188 (epub)
Subjects: LCSH: James, LeBron—Juvenile literature. I Forwards (Basketball)—Ohio—Biography—Juvenile literature. I African American basketball players—Ohio—Biography—Juvenile literature. I Basketball players—United States—Biography—Juvenile literature. I Cleveland Cavaliers (Basketball team)—Juvenile literature. I Miami Heat (Basketball team)—Juvenile literature. I Los Angeles Lakers (Basketball team)—Juvenile literature. I Black lives matter movement—Juvenile literature. I National Basketball Association—Juvenile literature.
Classification: LCC GV884.J36 A65 2024 (print) I LCC GV884.J36 (ebook) I DDC 796.323092 [B]—dc23/ eng/20240105

LC record available at https://lccn.loc.gov/2023051308
LC ebook record available at https://lccn.loc.gov/2023051309

Manufactured in the United States of America
1 – CG – 7/15/24

Table of Contents

CHAPTER 1
THE KID FROM AKRON

On December 30, 1984, Gloria James gave birth to a baby boy in Akron, Ohio. She named him LeBron. Only 16 years old, Gloria knew that raising a child of her own would be a challenge.

Luckily, Gloria could count on help from her own mother. Freda James Howard had raised Gloria and her two brothers.

I'm off to work. I love you all.

The family lived on what Freda earned as a hairstylist. There wasn't much money to go around. But there was always a lot of love.

When LeBron was three, Freda passed away from a heart attack. Gloria and her brothers knew they couldn't afford to keep living in the house without Freda's salary.

Gloria and LeBron were often unhoused. They slept at friends' houses or wherever they could find a warm bed. Because they moved around so much, LeBron often missed school.

But when LeBron was at school, he set himself apart through sports. He played basketball and football.

What a catch!

LeBron's quite the athlete.

Sure is, Coach Frank. But I heard from some of the boys that he hasn't been to school since before winter break.

That's not good.

Later, at Coach Frank Walker's house.

It's been really hard getting him to school. I'm taking whatever work I can, just trying to get us somewhere to live.

We believe in you both. And we want to help.

What if LeBron stays here during the week? Just until you find somewhere permanent to live. We'll make sure he gets to school. He can be with you on the weekends.

It was the hardest thing either of them ever had to do. But Gloria knew it would be the best for LeBron at the Walker home.

Okay.

LeBron didn't miss a single day of school during fifth grade. By the time he was in sixth grade, Gloria found an apartment for them both. But he stayed very close to the Walkers.

Around the same time, LeBron became a standout basketball player. Even he couldn't help remarking on his talent.

I'm so nice!

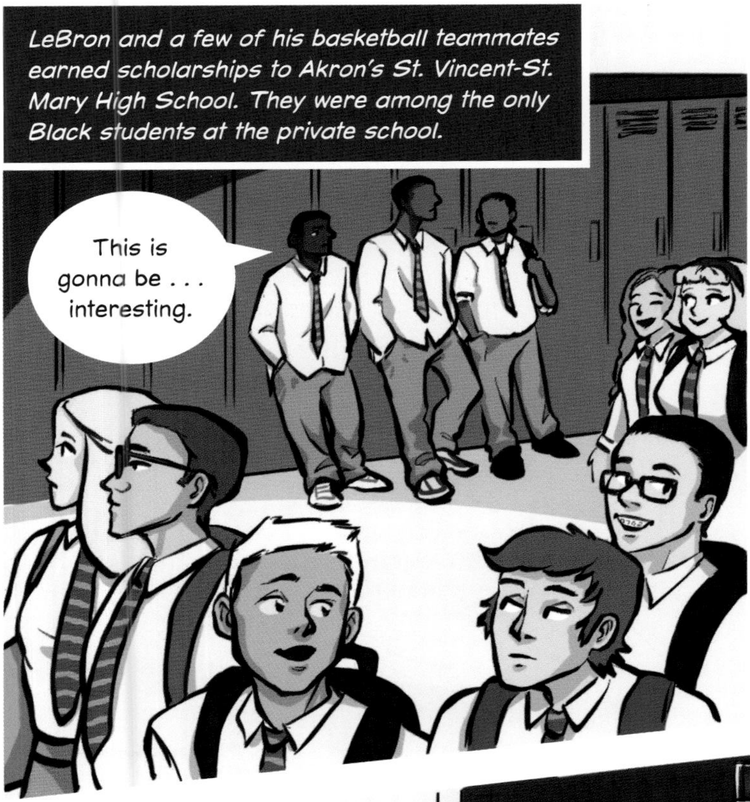
LeBron and a few of his basketball teammates earned scholarships to Akron's St. Vincent-St. Mary High School. They were among the only Black students at the private school.
This is gonna be . . . interesting.

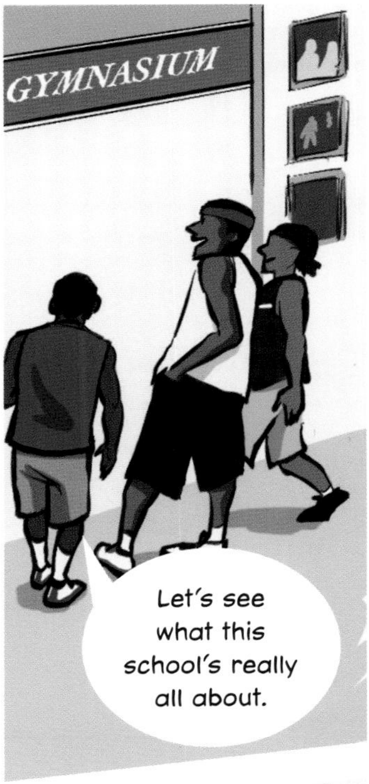
GYMNASIUM
Let's see what this school's really all about.

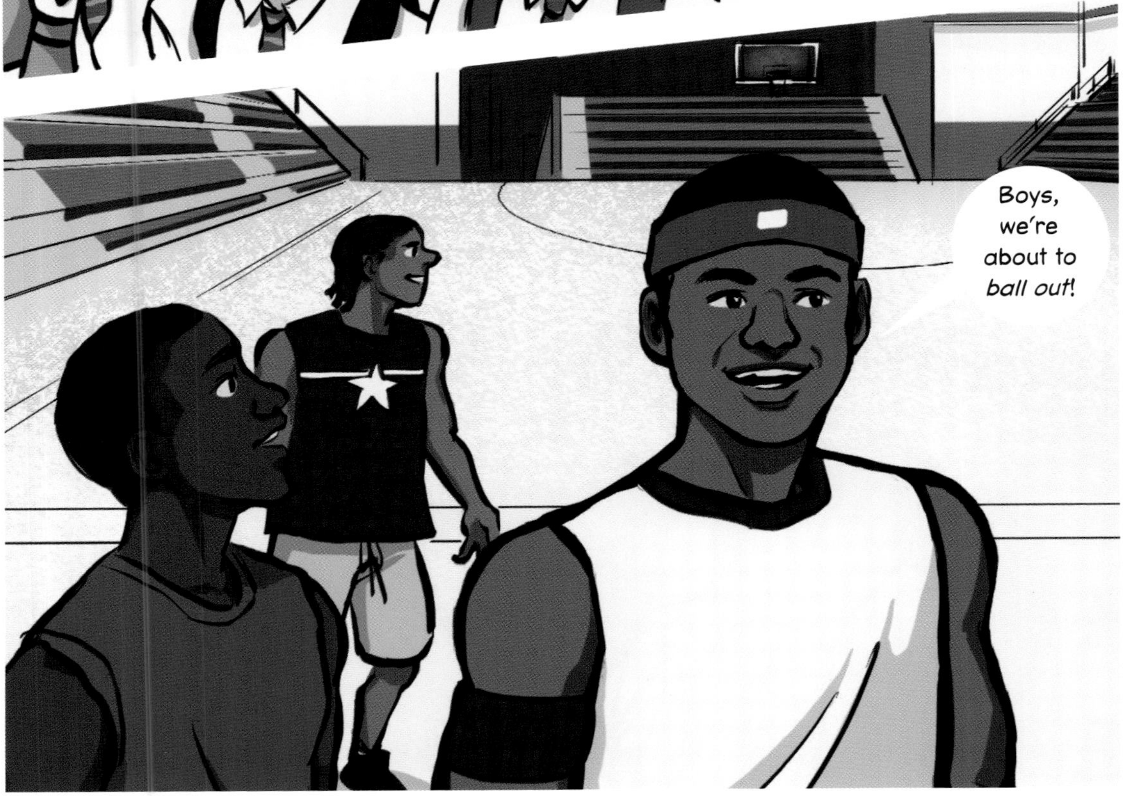
Boys, we're about to *ball out*!

CHAPTER 2
SUDDENLY A STAR

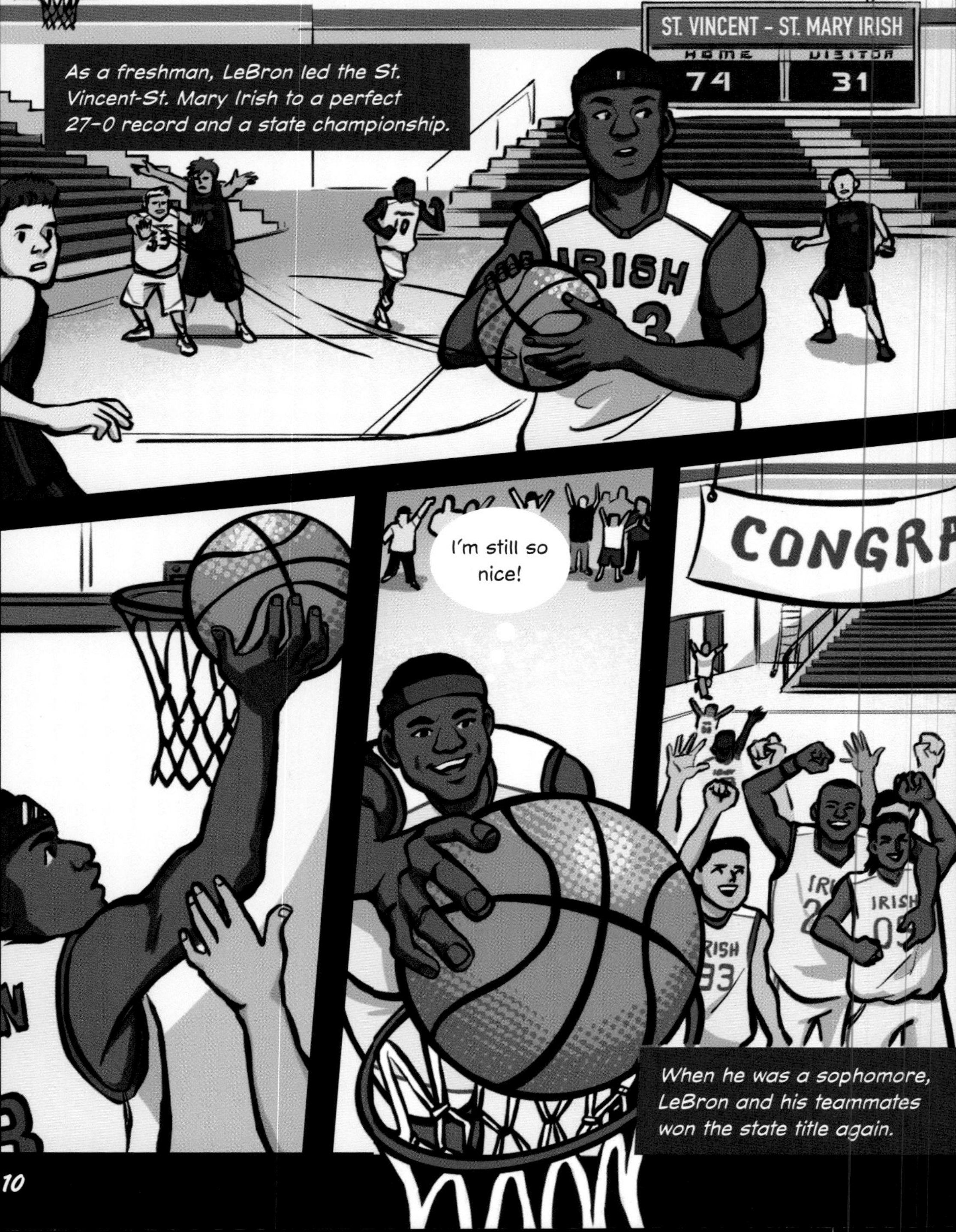
ST. VINCENT - ST. MARY IRISH
HOME
VISITOR
74
31
As a freshman, LeBron led the St. Vincent-St. Mary Irish to a perfect 27–0 record and a state championship.
I'm still so nice!
CONGR
When he was a sophomore, LeBron and his teammates won the state title again.

LeBron was the first sophomore ever to be named Mr. Basketball. The best high school player in Ohio receives this award.

Congratulations.

Thank you.

He got along well with his classmates, but sometimes he wondered . . .

Give it up for LeBron! He made *USA Today's* All-USA Basketball First Team!

Would they be so nice to me if I weren't such a good basketball player?

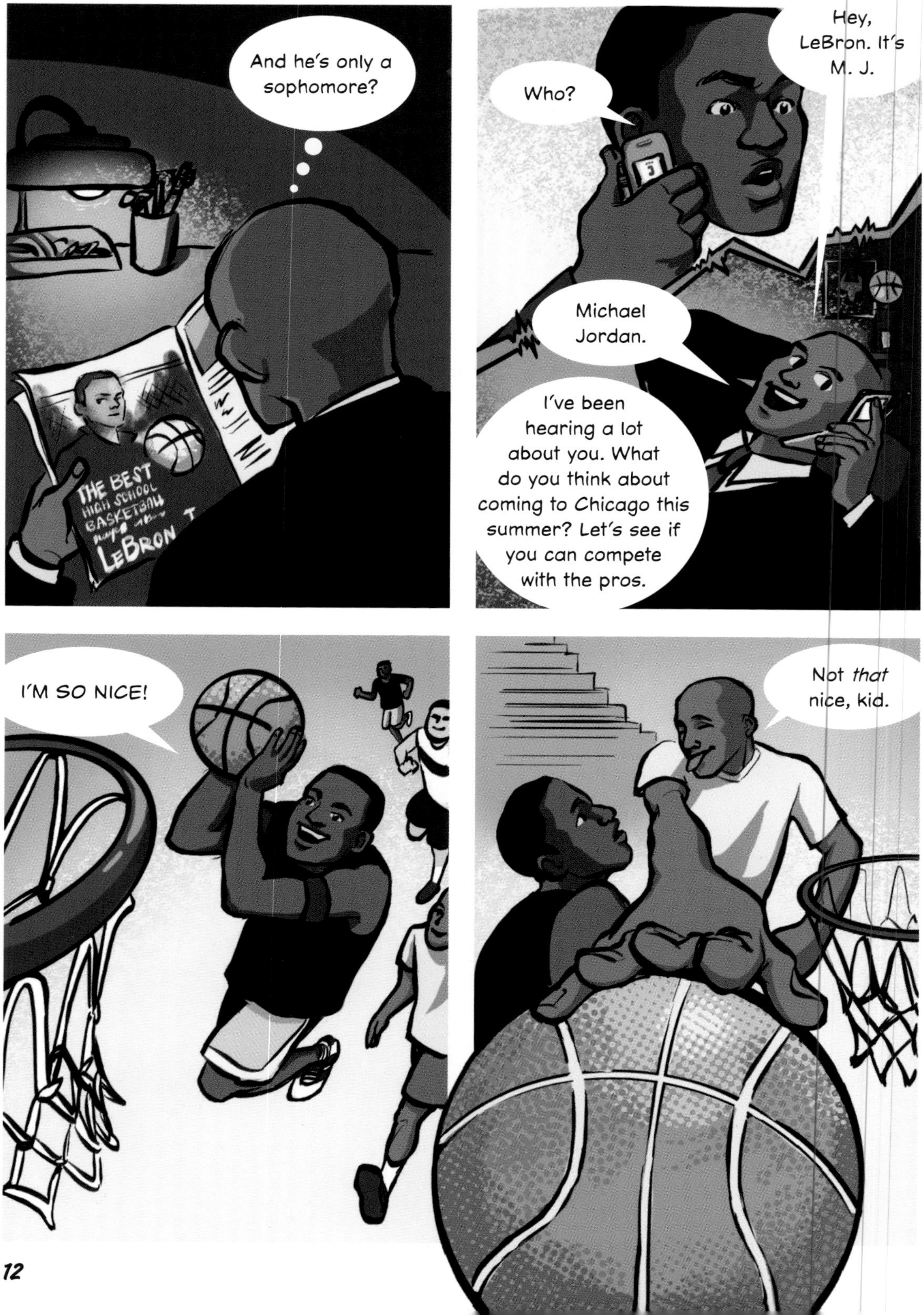
And he's only a sophomore?
THE BEST
HIGH SCHOOL
BASKETBALL
LeBRON
Hey, LeBron. It's M. J.
Who?
Michael Jordan.
I've been hearing a lot about you. What do you think about coming to Chicago this summer? Let's see if you can compete with the pros.
I'M SO NICE!
Not *that* nice, kid.

In 2002, LeBron became the first high school underclassman to appear on the cover of Sports Illustrated. Television networks aired many of his games.

Don't you read the news, man? You can't stop me . . . I'm the chosen one!

Remember when he used to be more humble?

He's got a big head . . .

Hey, LeBron, wanna hang with us?

I know I shouldn't, but . . .

Sometimes the pressure led him to make bad decisions. But LeBron was able to rely on support from friends and family. They kept him out of any serious trouble.

In 2003, the Irish captured their third state championship in four years. There was little room for argument: LeBron was ready for the NBA!

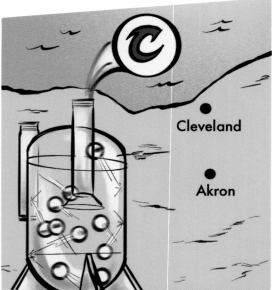

The Cleveland Cavaliers won the 2003 Draft Lottery. They got the first pick in the NBA Draft. Cleveland and Akron are neighboring Ohio cities. A 40-minute car ride is all that separates them.

June 26, 2003

With the first pick in the 2003 NBA Draft, the Cleveland Cavaliers select LeBron James.

Some players take a while to adjust to the speed of the NBA. LeBron fit in right away. The 2003–2004 Cavs won 18 more games than they had the season before. LeBron averaged 20 points per game. He took home the NBA's Rookie of the Year award.

From 2006 to 2010, LeBron led the Cavaliers to the playoffs five times. In 2007, they reached the NBA Finals. He won the NBA's Most Valuable Player award twice.

And it's *another* playoff loss for LeBron's Cavaliers.

But some people wondered whether he had the tools to win an NBA title.

After the 2010 playoffs, LeBron became a free agent. This meant he could choose to join any team in the league that offered him a contract. He loved playing close to home in Cleveland, but he craved more success for his team on the court.

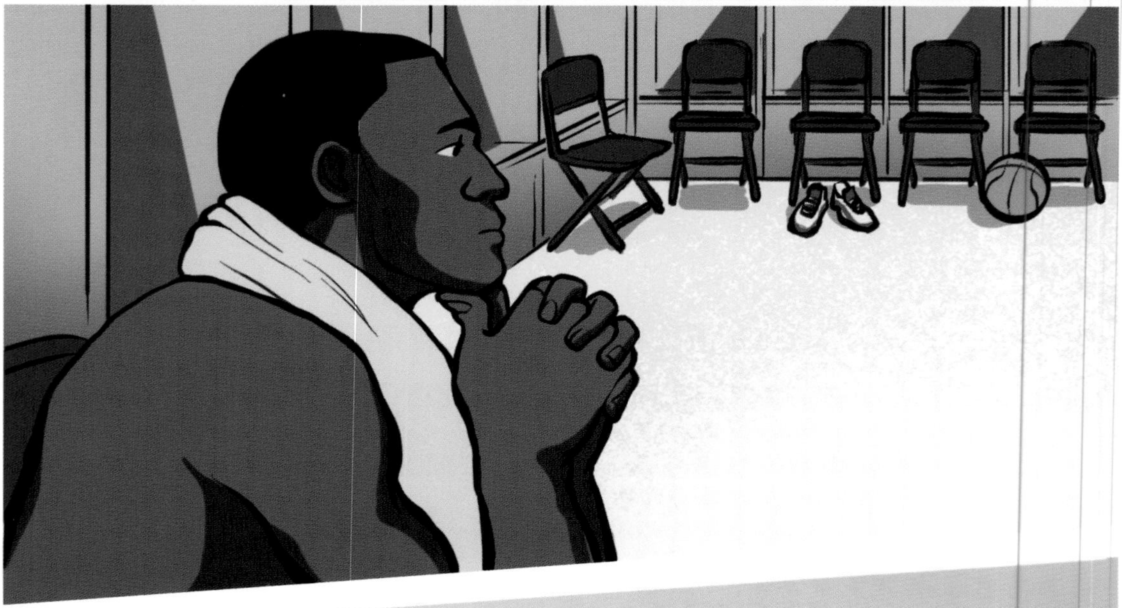

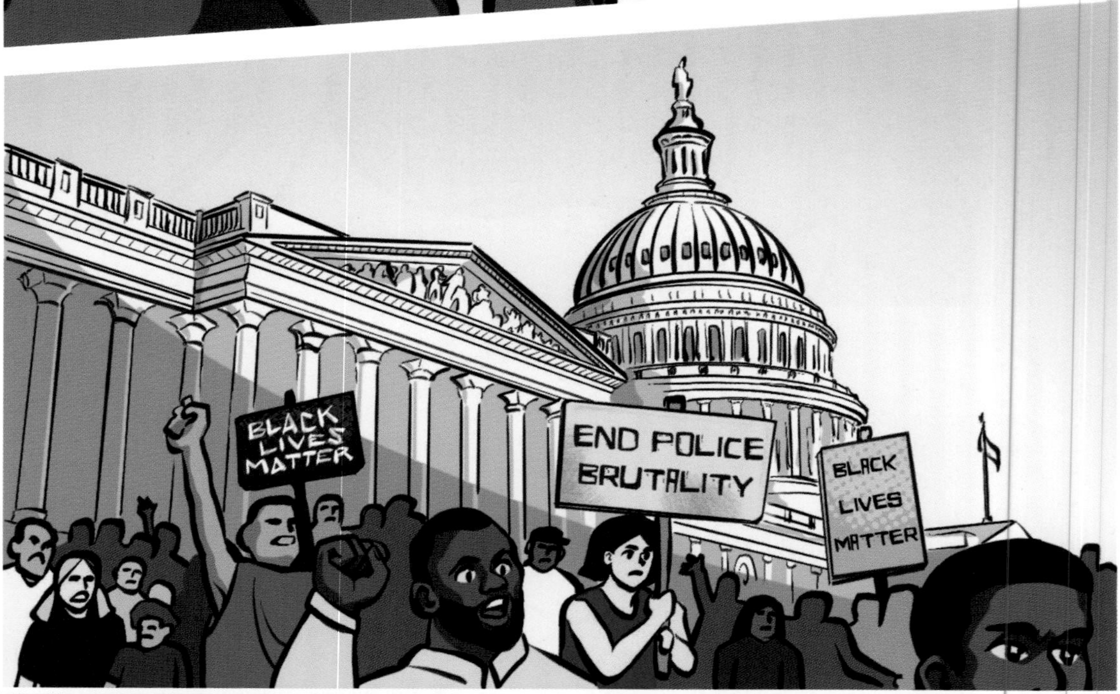
BLACK LIVES MATTER
END POLICE BRUTALITY
BLACK LIVES MATTER

LeBron was becoming one of the most famous people in the world. He knew he had a responsibility to speak up about issues related to the Black community. He craved a way to help others who might need it.

LeBron remembered how the Walker family helped him as a child. In 2004, he started the LeBron James Family Foundation.

In 2011, the Foundation opened the I PROMISE Program in Akron. At the time, around one-quarter of all students in Akron did not graduate from high school on time.

I PROMISE worked to help kids who were falling behind academically or socially. By 2018, they opened the I PROMISE School. I PROMISE aids around 1,500 kids every year.

CHAPTER 3
TITLE TIME

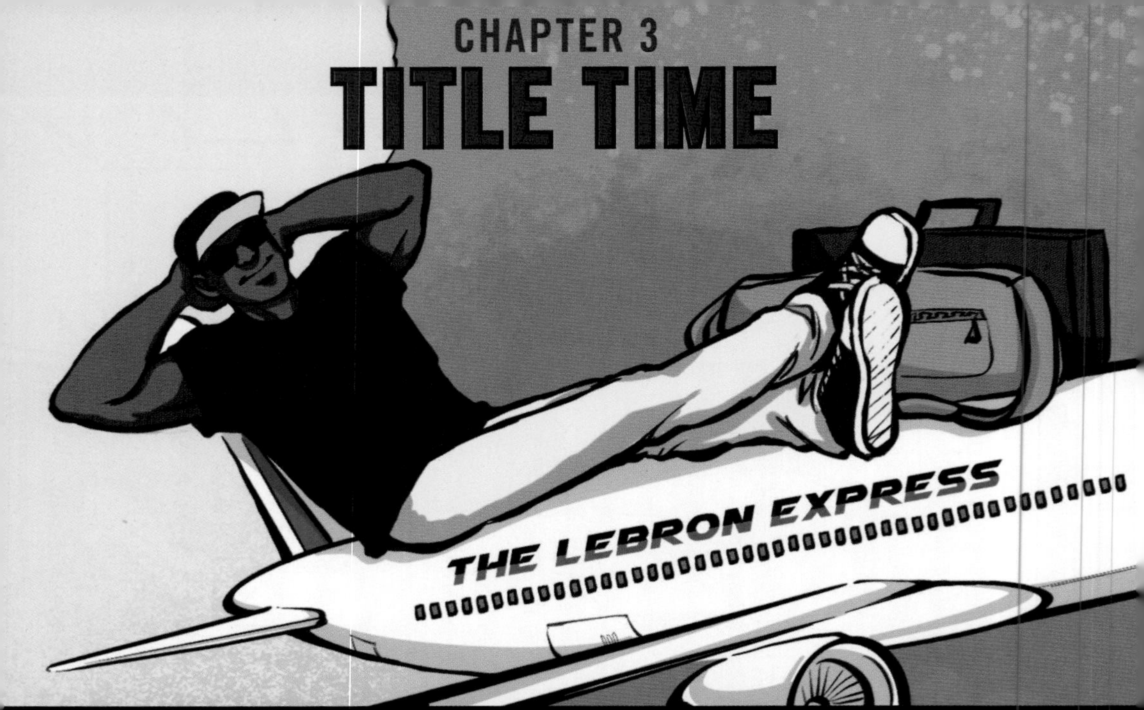
THE LEBRON EXPRESS

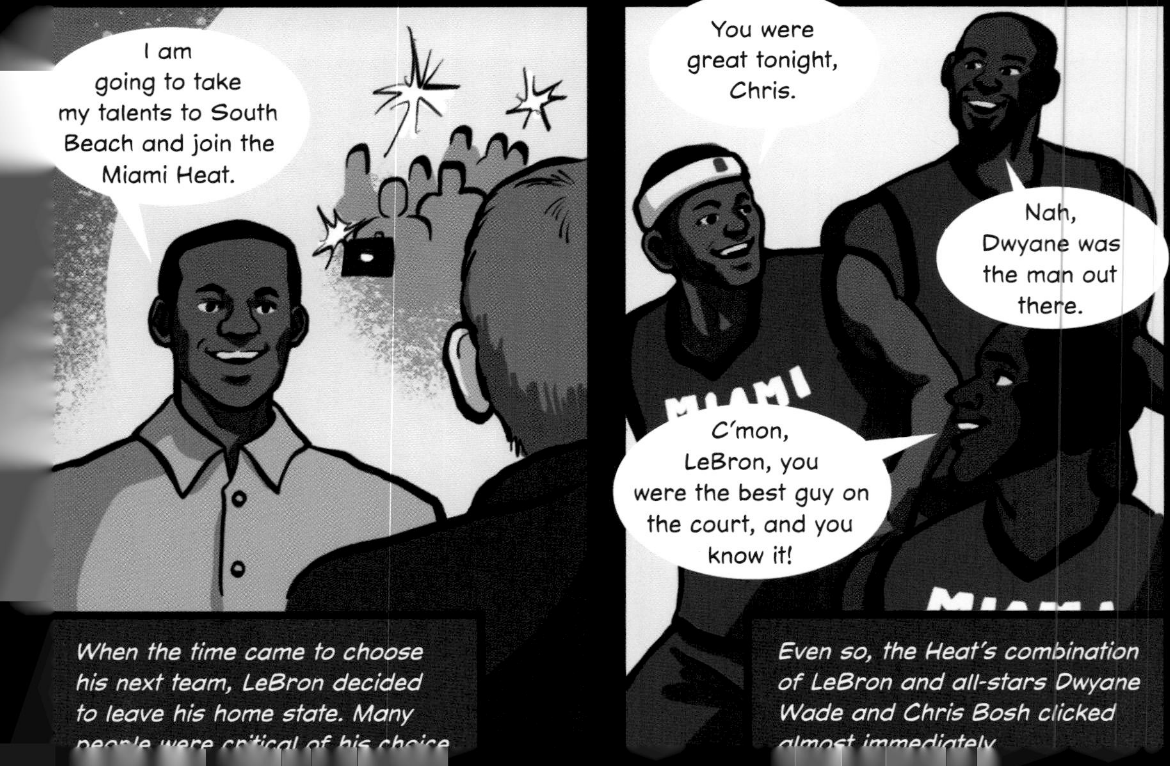
I am going to take my talents to South Beach and join the Miami Heat.
When the time came to choose his next team, LeBron decided to leave his home state. Many people were critical of his choice
You were great tonight, Chris.
Nah, Dwyane was the man out there.
C'mon, LeBron, you were the best guy on the court, and you know it!
MIAMI
Even so, the Heat's combination of LeBron and all-stars Dwyane Wade and Chris Bosh clicked almost immediately

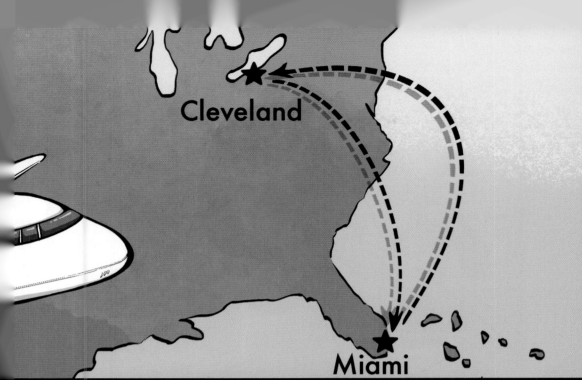

Cleveland

Miami

LeBron won two more MVP awards while playing for the Miami Heat.

In 2012, LeBron led the team to victory in the NBA Finals over the Oklahoma City Thunder. The Heat won the trophy the next year as well. No one would doubt again whether LeBron had what it took to win.

Hey, Mama, I'm home!

Even with his great success, LeBron felt he had unfinished business in Cleveland. He wanted to bring an NBA Championship home. After four seasons in Miami, he signed with the Cleveland Cavaliers again.

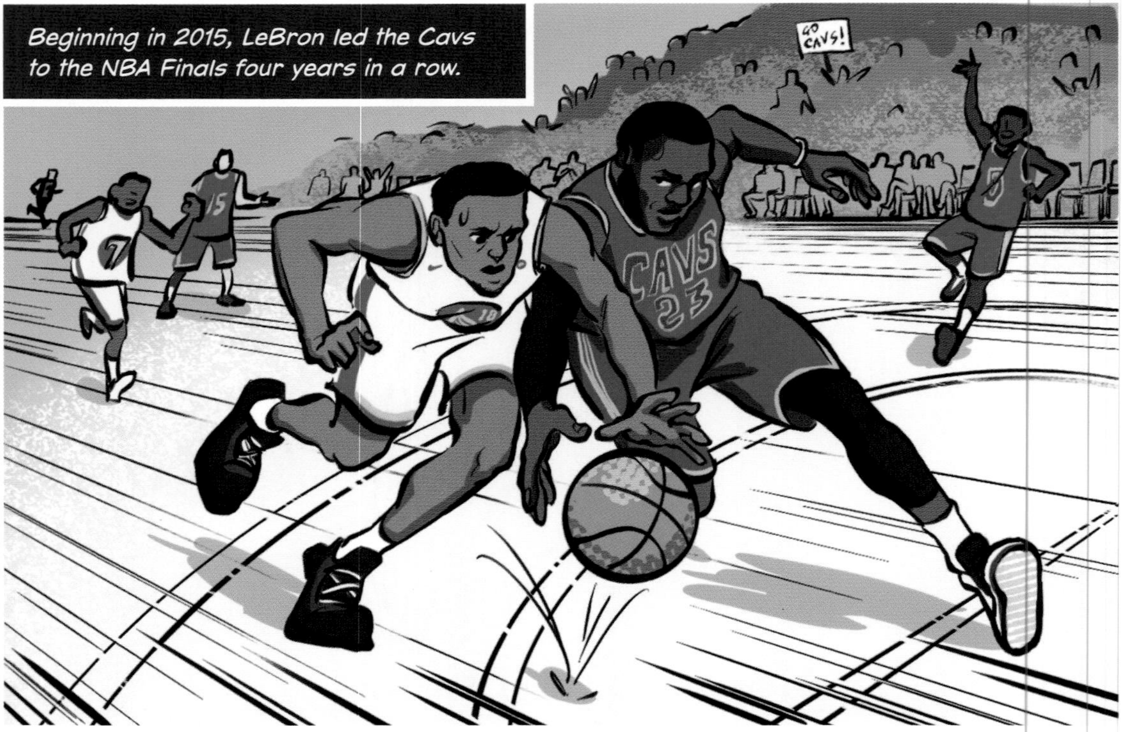
Beginning in 2015, LeBron led the Cavs to the NBA Finals four years in a row.
GO CAVS!
CAVS
23

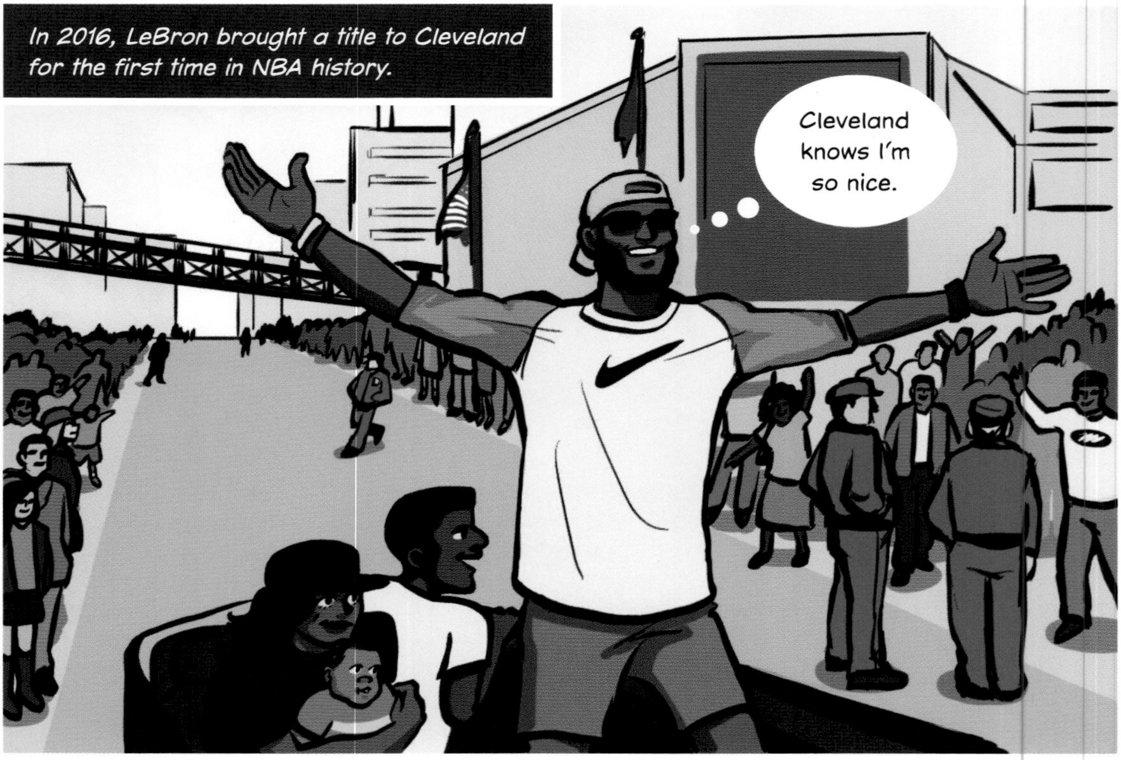
In 2016, LeBron brought a title to Cleveland for the first time in NBA history.
Cleveland knows I'm so nice.

Fame couldn't get him respect from everyone, though. LeBron came home one day to find his gate vandalized with a racist slur.

LeBron started speaking out more and more about the inequalities in America . . .

No matter how much money you have, no matter how famous you are, being Black in America is tough. . . . We got a long way to go for us . . . as African Americans until we feel equal in America.

. . . even though some criticized him for it.

LeBron should just shut up and dribble.

CHAPTER 4

DRIBBLING BUT NEVER STAYING SILENT

In 2020, a video spread around the country. It showed a police officer killing an unarmed Black man named George Floyd. Floyd was the latest Black person killed because of police brutality.

I can't breathe!

Police violence against Black Americans has been a problem for a long time. However, thanks to smartphones, it became more visible even before 2020.

Individuals such as Eric Garner, Michael Brown, Philando Castile, and Tyre Nichols are some of the most well-known victims of police brutality. Their cases provided strong examples of the systemic racism that exists within police forces in the United States.

I have to do something.

Black Man Shot During Traffic Stop

THE DAILY NEWS
Unarmed Black Man Killed In Ferguson

The New York Times
Cop Who Killed Garner Not Charged

Police

After Floyd's death, a movement called Black Lives Matter drove protests around the country. Protestors spoke out against violence toward Black people and racism in America.

The protests took place across the United States throughout the summer of 2020.

Meanwhile, the world tried to unite to fight the COVID-19 pandemic.

After pausing its season in March due to the virus, the NBA resumed play in July. All teams lived and played their games in "the bubble," an area in Orlando, Florida. Once inside, no one was allowed to leave without permission from the NBA.

By this point, LeBron was a member of the Los Angeles Lakers. Even from the bubble, he wanted to do something to show support for the protestors.

LeBron and other players made a joint statement. On July 30, 2020, they knelt during the national anthem.

LeBron became more and more outspoken about the need for change.

In August of 2020, police shot another Black man. This time, it was Jacob Blake of Kenosha, Wisconsin. He was seriously injured.

A new round of protests began.

NBA players organized a boycott and decided not to play. Games for the next few days were postponed.

We need to take a stand.

We can't go out there and play right now.

No way. Not until the league agrees to help.

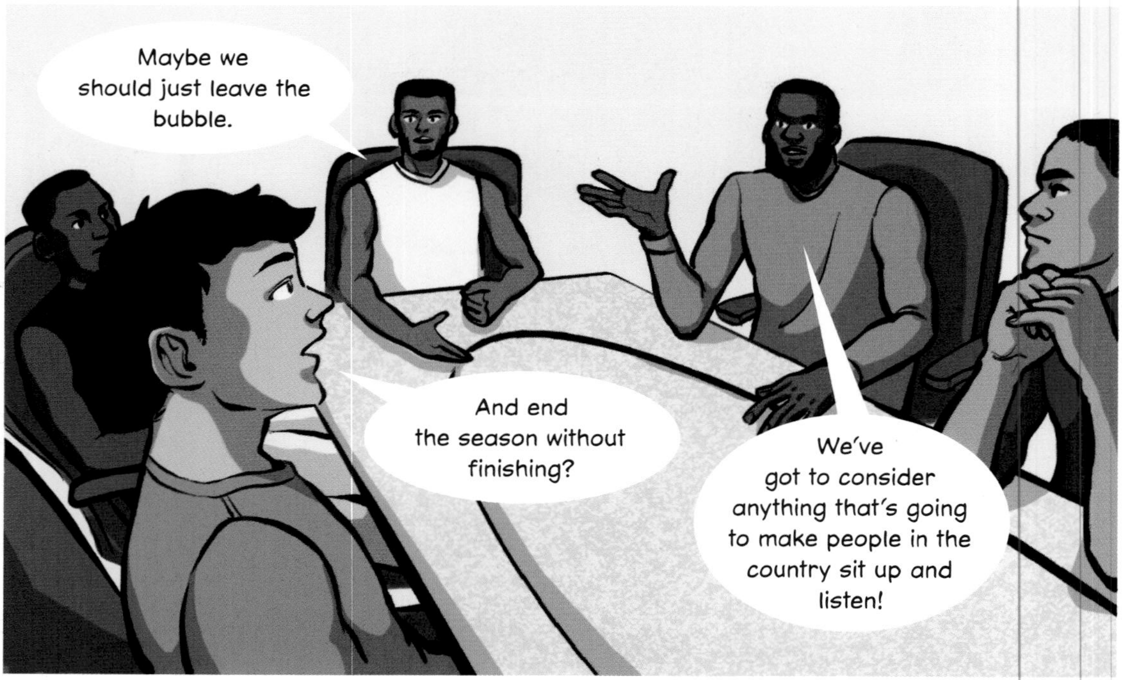
Maybe we should just leave the bubble.
And end the season without finishing?
We've got to consider anything that's going to make people in the country sit up and listen!

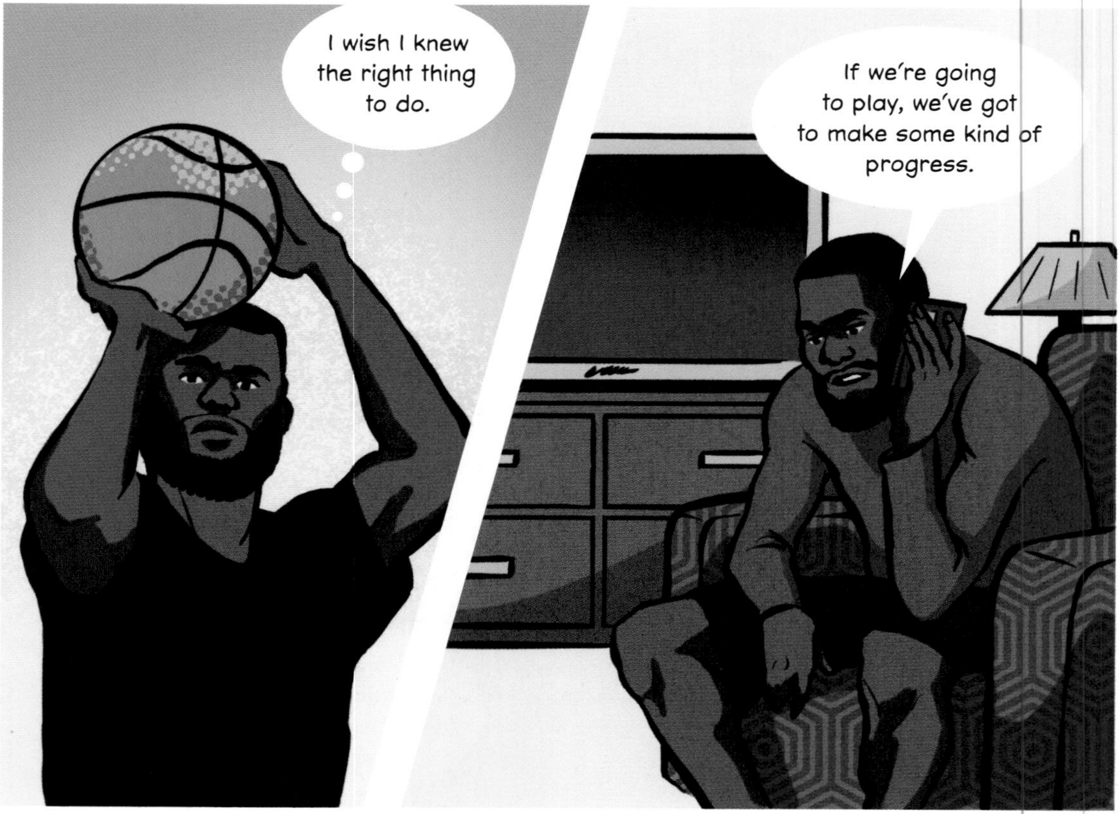
I wish I knew the right thing to do.
If we're going to play, we've got to make some kind of progress.

Two days later

The players are going to stay.

Players got several commitments from the NBA before finishing the season. One was that the league would open sports arenas as voting sites in November. Everyone should have the chance to vote on issues that affect them—including police reforms. With the league and players on the same page, the season went on.

LeBron led the Lakers to the NBA Finals against his old team, the Miami Heat.

LeBron dominated the series and won the Finals MVP award. He was only the fourth player to win an NBA title with three different teams.

AFTERWORD

LeBron refused to just "shut up and dribble." In 2022, he spoke out when the Supreme Court overturned Roe v. Wade. This decision reduced a woman's reproductive freedoms. He argued that the decision was about "power and control."

The LeBron James Family Foundation continues to help more and more children and families around Akron, Ohio. The Foundation has opened a medical facility and a workforce training center. It also oversees transitional housing. This service helps families impacted by challenges like the ones LeBron's mother faced when he was a child.

In November 2023, LeBron became the first NBA player in history to score more than 39,000 points. Only six other players have surpassed 30,000. That same month, he became the all-time leader in minutes played, with 66,319 minutes spent on the court.

Even though he's accomplished almost everything there is to accomplish on a basketball court, LeBron has one more NBA goal. He hopes to keep playing long enough to be on the same team with his sons, Bronny and Bryce. Both could be eligible for the NBA Draft in the next few years.

ATHLETE SNAPSHOT

BIRTH NAME: LeBron Raymone James

NICKNAME: King James

BORN: December 30, 1984

- ◆ 2004—NBA Rookie of the Year
- ◆ 2004—Olympic bronze medal winner
- ◆ 2008, 2012—Olympic gold medal winner
- ◆ 2009, 2010, 2012, 2013—NBA Most Valuable Player award
- ◆ 2023—Leading scorer in the history of the NBA, with 38,390 career points

SOURCE NOTES

18   Julian Linden. "LeBron James Joims the Heat in Search of Elusive Title." *Reuters*, July 8, 2010, https://www.reuters.com/article/uk-nba-james-idUKTRE6680CP20100709/

21   Adam Wells, "LeBron James Says Racists Don't Care How Much Money He Has," *Bleacher Report*, February 15, 2018, https://bleacherreport.com/articles/2759712-lebron-james-says-racists-dont-care-how-much-money-he-has

21   Emily Sullivan, "Laura Ingraham Told LeBron James to Shut Up and Dribble; He Went to the Hoop," *NPR*, February 19, 2018, https://www.npr.org/sections/thetwo-way/2018/02/19/587097707/laura-ingraham-told-lebron-james-to-shutup-and-dribble-he-went-to-the-hoop

GLOSSARY

draft: an event in which athletes are picked to join sports organizations or teams

foundation: an organization that gives money to good causes

humble: being modest

playoffs: a series of games played after the regular season to determine a champion

police brutality: the act of a police officer using more force than necessary

protest: to object to something strongly and publicly

reform: to make or bring about social or political changes

scholarship: money given to a student to pay for school

slur: insulting name or word

systemic racism: harmful or unfair actions based on race or ethnicity that exists throughout a whole society

unhoused: having no place to live

FURTHER INFORMATION

BLM Resources for Kids
https://www.museumofsocialjustice.org/blm-resources-for-kids.html

Britannica Kids: Homelessness
https://kids.britannica.com/students/article/homelessness/274923

Downs, Kevin. *LeBron James*. Minneapolis: Bellwether Media, 2023.

Greenberg, Keith Elliot. *LeBron vs. Michael Jordan: Who Would Win?*
Minneapolis: Lerner Publications, 2024.

LeBron James Family Foundation
https://www.lebronjamesfamilyfoundation.org/

LeBron James
https://www.lebronjames.com/

INDEX